Veggie
MANIA ®

Cathy Prange and Joan Pauli

Macmillan Canada

Toronto

Veggie Mania®
by Cathy Prange and Joan Pauli
Copyright © 1986, 1998

Canadian Cataloguing in Publication Data

Prange, Cathy, 1931–
Veggie mania

ISBN 0-7715-7559-9

1. Cookery (Vegetables). I. Pauli, Joan, 1937–   . II. Title

TX801.P73 1998   641.6'5   C97-932157-3

1 2 3 4 5 TRI 02 01 00 99 98

This book is available at special discounts for bulk purchases by your
group or organization for sales promotions, premiums, fundraising and
seminars. For details, contact: Macmillan Canada, Special Sales Department,
29 Birch Avenue, Toronto, ON M4V 1E2. Tel: 416-963-8830.

Pictured on cover: Eggplant Parmesan, 48
Photography: Hal Roth
Photo Assistant: Andrew Tomkins
Food Stylist: Lasha Andrushko

Macmillan Canada
A Division of Canada Publishing Corporation
Toronto, Ontario, Canada

Printed in Canada

The original introduction to *Veggie Mania*
when it was first published:

You loved our muffins,
You loved our nibbles,
You'll love our veggies too!
Our book is filled
With garden greens,
And they are good for you!

Can you believe this? Now we are writing poetry! But that doesn't mean we're tired of making muffins and nibbles—it's still great fun! This just seemed to be a good way to introduce our new book, *Veggie Mania*.

Many of you have been asking, "What's next?" Well, here it is! Your tremendous support over the last four years has forced us out of the office and back into the kitchen (only kidding, we never really left!). Instead of spending *all* Friday morning in the kitchen, we are now in the supermarkets, hovering around the produce counters and filling our carts with veggies.

Our Research Department (which consists of us) has worked very hard to determine the biggest meal-time dilemma, and the resounding response was "veggies!" Therefore, in keeping with today's lifestyle, we have tried to give you delicious, easy to prepare recipes. With two Canadian bestsellers and *La Manie des Muffins,* it is more important than ever to be organized!

Have a meal plan like a game plan! Why be stuck in the kitchen, missing the fun (and cocktails)? After all, guests do not feel comfortable entertaining themselves.

You'll love our *Veggie Mania*! There is a vegetable for everyone's taste and for every occasion.

We had fun doing it! You'll have fun using it!

Sisters, Partners and Still Best Friends,
Cathy Prange
Joan Pauli

HINTS

Eat, drink and be merry
Is a symptom of our day,
Be sure of healthy eating
The *Veggie Mania* way!

1. Most of our top-of-the-stove veggies may be made ahead, placed in a greased casserole and reheated in your oven or microwave.

2. It is easier and more economical to substitute powdered chicken or beef broth for canned broth.

3. To gild a lily, pour a little melted butter and grated lemon rind over cooked fresh veggies.

4. Mix left-over mashed potatoes with an egg and 1 tbsp. flour, roll in cereal crumbs and chill on a greased cookie sheet until ready to bake. Tastes better than a mashed potato sandwich!

5. Remember, our lunch or brunch muffins will complement your soups and salads!

6. If you have peeled more potatoes than you want to cook, cover them with some water with a few drops of vinegar added. They will keep 3 or 4 days in your refrigerator.

7. Never discard parsley or celery leaves. Remove all branches and dehydrate in microwave for 4 min., turning once. Crumble and store in covered jar. Use as a garnish and as a flavouring in soups and stews.

CONTENTS

Soups

Salads

Hot Veggie Combos

Soups

Soups, salads and make-aheads
Are oh so easy to do,
And the best part of our veggie book
Is that they are *good* for you!

Doris's Borscht

2-½ lb. spare ribs
3 c. sliced beets, cut into strips
2 c. beet leaves and stems, cut up
2 c. shredded red or green cabbage
1 medium carrot, sliced
1 stalk celery (¾ c. with a few leaves)
1 large onion, chopped
1 c. canned tomatoes or 1 c. fresh
1 clove garlic, crushed
1 tsp. chopped parsley
1 tsp. chopped dill weed
3 tsp. salt
½ tsp. pepper
2-½ tsp. white vinegar
2 tbsp. flour
2 tbsp. butter
1 c. sour cream

Boil ribs for 3 min. Drain and rinse in cold water.

Now we start the borscht. Bring 12 c. of water to a boil, drop
in the ribs and boil for 5 min. Add all the ingredients except
the flour, butter and sour cream.

Boil until the spare ribs are nearly tender and then lower heat.

Melt the butter on low heat in a frying pan and add flour,
stirring, until light brown. Add 2 c. of soup to this mixture
and boil a few minutes. Add to the pot of soup while it is
boiling on low heat and boil about 3 min. longer. Let the
soup cool.

Take 2 c. of soup and put it into another pot. Cool completely. Add the sour cream to this, blending it together. A tablespoon of milk will help to blend it.

Add this to the cooled soup. The soup should not be boiled after the sour cream mixture has been added. Heat and serve.

This soup tastes much better after it has been sitting aside for 6 hrs. It even tastes better the next day.

Note

You will notice throughout the method that cooled soup is mentioned several times. Cooling the soup prevents curdling.

This borscht tastes best when fresh beets are used; it also freezes well.

You won't believe what a delicious "one-pot meal" this hot soup is!

To serve, remove ribs and serve on the side!

Cabbage Soup

---

1 lb. ground beef
1 medium onion, chopped
½ c. diced celery
½ green pepper, chopped
2 tbsp. oil
2 tsp. salt
2 tbsp. white sugar
¼ tsp. pepper
dash paprika
1 can (28 oz.) tomatoes
2 cans (each 5-½ oz.) tomato paste
4 c. hot water
2 beef bouillon cubes
3 tbsp. parsley flakes
1 large potato, diced
2 medium carrots, diced
1 small head cabbage, coarsely chopped

In large soup pot, sauté ground beef, onion, celery and green pepper in oil until beef is browned (breaking up while browning).

Add remaining ingredients except cabbage and combine thoroughly. Simmer, uncovered, for 1 hr., stirring occasionally.

Add cabbage. Combine and simmer, covered, for 1 hr.

If too thick, add more hot water.

A good, nutritious meal in a bowl!

Louise's Cream of Carrot Soup

½ c. chopped onions
⅓ c. butter
2 c. sliced medium carrots (3 med.)
3 chicken bouillon cubes
3 c. boiling water
¼ c. rice
½ tsp. salt
2 c. milk

Sauté onions in butter until transparent.

Add carrots and stir until well coated.

Add bouillon cubes, water, rice and salt. Cook until rice and carrots are tender, about 20 min.

Place in blender and purée.

(Soup can be made ahead to this point and refrigerated.)

When ready to serve, return to pot, add milk and heat.

Cream of Cauliflower Soup

1 large onion
2 tbsp. butter or margarine
3 cans chicken broth
2 medium carrots, sliced
1 medium cauliflower, cut into pieces
1 c. heavy cream
salt and pepper to taste
⅛ tsp. nutmeg
1 tbsp. sherry
parsley for garnish

Slice onion and sauté in butter or margarine in large saucepan until limp, about 5 min.

Add chicken broth and bring to a boil. Add carrots and cauliflower to boiling broth and simmer, covered, until veggies are tender, about 15 min.

Purée in blender or food processor.

Return to soup pot and add cream, salt, pepper, nutmeg and sherry. Heat, but do not boil.

Garnish with parsley, croutons or tiny cauliflowerets.

Serves 6–8.

Just as delicious when broccoli or asparagus is substituted for cauliflower!

Donna's Corn Chowder

1 c. chopped onion
2 tbsp. butter
2 cooked potatoes, diced
2 c. ground or chopped ham
1 can (19 oz.) creamed corn
1 can cream of mushroom soup
2-½ c. milk
¾ tsp. salt

Sauté onion in butter in saucepan.

Add rest of ingredients and heat just to boiling.

Use your left-over ham or 1 can flaked ham in this easy chowder. Men love this one!

For making corn-on-the-cob that stays hot and fresh, use only cold water and, for every 4 ears, 2 tbsp. each of sugar and vinegar. Bring water to a boil, then add corn. Cook for 6 min. and then remove the corn as desired. The corn left simmering in the hot water will stay fresh for hours!

Fresh Mushroom Soup

4 slices bacon, cut into small pieces
3 tbsp. butter
1 large onion, chopped
2 cloves garlic, minced
2 lb. mushrooms, sliced
6 tbsp. tomato paste
6 c. chicken broth
4 tbsp. sweet vermouth or sherry
1 tsp. salt
½ tsp. freshly ground pepper
grated mozzarella, swiss or parmesan cheese

Cook bacon until brown. Add butter.

Add onion and garlic, and cook until soft.

Stir in mushrooms and cook gently for 10 min.

Stir in tomato paste.

Add chicken broth, vermouth or sherry, salt and pepper. Simmer for 10 min.

Pour into soup bowls and sprinkle with cheese.

Serves 6.

Serve as a change from French Onion Soup!

French Onion Soup

6 medium onions, thinly sliced
6 tbsp. butter
1 tsp. white sugar
1 tsp. salt
dash nutmeg
7 c. beef broth
¼ c. sherry
6 slices of French bread, toasted,
    or 6 Holland rusks
grated swiss cheese
grated parmesan cheese

Sauté onion in butter until soft.

Add sugar, salt and nutmeg and toss well.

Cook until golden brown. Add broth and bring to a boil.

Simmer 10 min. and add sherry.

Ladle soup into oven-proof bowls and top with a slice of toasted French bread or a Holland rusk.

Cover with swiss cheese.

Bake at 300 degrees for 10 min.

Add parmesan and broil until cheese bubbles.

Serves 6.

You don't have to be French to like this one!

Potato Leek Soup

1-½ c. diced leeks (approx. 2)
½ c. diced onion
1 clove garlic, minced
4 tbsp. butter
4 c. chicken broth
1-½ c. diced potatoes
1 c. heavy cream
salt and pepper to taste
chopped green onions

Sauté leeks, onion and garlic in butter until transparent.

Add broth and potatoes and bring to a boil. Cover and simmer until potatoes are tender, about 15 min.

Purée in blender or food processor.

Return to large saucepan and add cream, salt and pepper.

(If soup is too thick, add more cream or broth.)

Garnish with chopped green onions.

Serves 8.

A tasty prelude to your gourmet dinner. Delicious hot or cold.

Salads

Three Bean Salad

---

1 can (14 oz.) green beans
1 can (14 oz.) yellow beans
1 can (14 oz.) kidney beans
1 can (19 oz.) chick peas
¾ c. white sugar
⅔ c. white vinegar
½ c. oil
1 tsp. salt
½ tsp. pepper
1 medium onion, chopped
1 green pepper, cut in small pieces

Drain the beans and the chick peas. In a small bowl, mix the sugar, vinegar, oil, salt and pepper.

In a large bowl, mix the drained beans and chick peas, chopped onion, green pepper and the marinade.

Refrigerate one day before use.

Store in covered jars in the refrigerator.

Drain before serving.

An all-time favourite for any occasion. An easy make-ahead that complements any meal.
Take to your next pot luck supper!

Beet Mold

---

    1 can (14 oz.) crushed pineapple
    1 can (14 oz.) diced harvard beets
    3 tbsp. white vinegar
    1 tsp. onion salt
    2 small pkg. Wild Cherry Jell-O

Drain juice from pineapple and beets. Add water to juice, if necessary, to make 3 c. of liquid.

In medium saucepan, heat the juice, vinegar and onion salt.

Stir in and dissolve the 2 pkg. of Wild Cherry Jell-O.

Chill juice until slightly thickened and then add pineapple and beets.

Pour into bowl or mold and let set.

We find this colourful mold is delicious served with any meat.
Try this instead of cranberries with your roast turkey or chicken!

Janie's Broccoli Salad

1 bunch broccoli, cut into spears
½ lb. bacon, cooked, drained and crumbled
1 c. grated cheddar cheese
1 large onion, chopped, or 4 green onions, chopped

Dressing:
1 c. salad cream
¼ c. white sugar
2 tbsp. white vinegar

Mix together broccoli, bacon, cheddar cheese and onion.

In a small bowl, combine dressing ingredients.

Toss with vegetables.

Serves 6–8.

If you're bored with cabbage salad, try this!
Certainly a hit with our family and guests.

Mother Milner's Horseradish Mold

1 pkg. unflavoured gelatin
¼ c. cold water
¼ c. hot water
½ c. sweet pickle juice
2 tbsp. lemon juice
½ c. horseradish, drained
½ c. mayonnaise
½ c. chopped celery

Dissolve gelatin in cold water.

Add hot water.

Add pickle juice, lemon juice and horseradish. Allow to partially set.

When partially set, fold in mayonnaise and celery.

Pour into mold or glass dish.

No sneezing at your dinner table with this one!
A super, mild accompaniment for your roast beef!

Layered 24-Hour Veggie Salad

1 head lettuce, torn
1 tsp. white sugar
salt and pepper to taste
6 hard-cooked eggs, sliced
1 pkg. (10 oz.) frozen peas, thawed
1 lb. bacon, cooked, drained and crumbled
2 c. grated swiss cheese
1 c. mayonnaise or salad cream
sliced green onions with tops (optional)

In bottom of large salad bowl, place 3 c. of torn lettuce. Sprinkle with sugar, salt and pepper.

Layer sliced eggs on top of lettuce, standing some slices around edge of bowl. Sprinkle with a little salt.

Next, layer in order: peas, remaining lettuce, bacon and swiss cheese.

Gently spread mayonnaise or salad cream over the top, sealing to the edge of the bowl.

Cover and refrigerate 24 hrs. or overnight.

Garnish with green onions, if desired.

Toss just before serving.

Serves 12–15.

Make-Ahead Layered Salad

1 head lettuce, torn
½ head cauliflower, broken into bite-size pieces
1 lb. bacon, cooked, drained and crumbled
3 medium green onions, chopped
2 c. salad cream
¼ c. white sugar
⅓ c. grated parmesan cheese

Layer lettuce, cauliflower, bacon and green onion in large salad bowl.

Mix salad cream with sugar and parmesan cheese. Spread over greens and seal to edge of bowl.

Refrigerate overnight and toss just before serving.

Serves 10.

Both our make-ahead layered salads are great for your buffets, or for salad lovers, they're a meal by themselves served with hot luncheon muffins!

Julia's Fresh Mushroom Salad

1 head romaine
1 head lettuce
½ lb. mushrooms

Dressing
½ c. oil
¼ c. white vinegar
¼ c. chopped green onion
¼ c. chopped parsley
1 tbsp. chopped green pepper
1 tsp. white sugar
1 tsp. salt
1 tsp. dry mustard
⅛ tsp. cayenne

Line a salad bowl with romaine leaves.

Tear rest of romaine and head lettuce into bite-size pieces.

Wash, trim and slice mushrooms, and combine with lettuce.

Beat all dressing ingredients with beater or shake well in tightly covered jar. Store in refrigerator.

Shake well before tossing with lettuce and mushrooms and serving.

Serves 4–6.

Ladies! A great luncheon salad!

Maureen's Dilly Onion Rings

⅓ c. white sugar
2 tsp. salt
1 tsp. dill weed
½ c. white vinegar
¼ c. water
1 large Spanish onion, thinly sliced
   and separated into rings

Combine all ingredients except onion.

Stir until sugar dissolves.

Pour over onion rings, cover and refrigerate at least 5 hrs.

Stir occasionally.

(May be made 1 or 2 days before needed.)

Drain and serve.

This recipe takes the "hot" out of onions. A super side dish for special occasions or your family barbecue.

Sauerkraut Salad

---

1 can (28 oz.) sauerkraut, drained
1 can (19 oz.) bean sprouts, drained
2 c. celery, chopped
1 green pepper, chopped
1 pimiento, chopped
1 c. white vinegar
1 c. white sugar

Mix all ingredients except vinegar and sugar.

Boil vinegar and sugar for 3 min., cool and pour over sauerkraut and vegetables.

Refrigerate, covered, until ready to use.

Keeps well.

Another Waterloo County favourite! Even if you don't like sauerkraut, you'll love this!

Marinated Veggies (1)

1 can baby carrots, drained
1 green pepper, sliced in rings
1 large red onion, sliced in rings
½ lb. mushrooms, washed and drained well,
  or 1 can whole mushrooms, drained
1 cucumber, pared and sliced
1 small bottle Italian dressing

Combine veggies and toss with dressing.

Marinate at least 6 hrs. or overnight.

Drain and serve.

A vegetable a day keeps the doctor's bills away!

Variation
Instead of bottled Italian dressing, use 1 pkg. Italian dressing
mixed with 2 tbsp. sugar, 2 tbsp. salad oil and 2 tbsp. tarragon
vinegar.

Marinated Veggies (2)

1 bunch broccoli, washed and cut into spears
1 small cauliflower, cleaned and cut into
   bite-size pieces
1 can whole mushrooms, drained
1 green pepper, sliced
cherry tomatoes
1 large bottle Italian dressing

Place veggies in large bowl and pour dressing over all.

Cover and refrigerate overnight.

Drain and serve.

A colourful side dish for lunch or dinner parties!

Hot Veggie Combos

Simple and Delicious Veggie Topping

½ c. butter
1 small onion, grated
1 c. mayonnaise
1 tbsp. horseradish
1 tbsp. prepared mustard
1 tsp. salt
black pepper or cayenne to taste

Allow butter and onion to soften together. (Do not melt.)

Add remaining ingredients.

Mix well and refrigerate.

Keeps in refrigerator for a remarkable time.
"Great served over fresh broccoli and asparagus!"

To soften hard butter in a hurry, grate it!

Asparagus Casserole

Cream Sauce:
2 tbsp. butter or margarine
2 tbsp. flour
½ tsp. salt
dash pepper
½ tsp. curry powder
2 c. milk
2 cans (each 12 oz.) asparagus tips
    or 2 lb. fresh, cooked
5 hard-cooked eggs, sliced
½ c. grated cheddar cheese

Buttered Crumbs
1 c. dry bread crumbs or cracker crumbs
2 tbsp. butter, melted

Melt butter or margarine and blend in flour, salt, pepper and curry powder. Add milk and cook stirring constantly, until mixture thickens.

Layer asparagus, eggs, cheese and cream sauce.

Top with buttered crumbs.

Bake in a casserole at 350 degrees for 30 min. or until hot and bubbly.

Serves 6.

No Crust, No Fuss Asparagus Quiche

1 lb. asparagus
2 tbsp. soft butter
¼ c. fine, dry bread crumbs
8 slices bacon or 1 c. diced cooked ham
1 c. grated Fontina or cheddar cheese
3 eggs
1 c. light cream
½ c. milk
pinch nutmeg
freshly ground pepper

Cut asparagus into 2-in. lengths. Cook in boiling salted water until tender-crisp. Drain well.

Spread bottom and sides of a 10-in. quiche dish with the butter.

Sprinkle the bread crumbs on top and make sure bottom and sides of dish are coated.

Cook bacon until crisp, drain and crumble. Sprinkle bacon or ham over the crumbs.

Sprinkle ¾ c. of cheese over bacon.

Arrange asparagus over cheese, reserving 6 of the tips for the top.

Beat eggs, cream, milk and seasonings and pour over all. Top with rest of the cheese.

Decorate top with reserved asparagus tips. Bake at 350 degrees for 40–45 min.

Bar-Room Casserole
(Barley Mushroom Casserole)

¼ c. butter or margarine
½ lb. mushrooms, thinly sliced
1 large onion, coarsely chopped
1 c. pearl barley
½ tsp. salt
⅛ tsp. pepper
4 c. chicken broth

Melt butter or margarine and sauté mushrooms and onion for 5 min. or until tender.

Add barley and brown slightly, stirring frequently. Stir in salt and pepper and turn into a 2-qt. casserole.

Add chicken broth and mix well.

Cover and bake at 350 degrees for 1-½ hrs. Add more broth, if needed.

Serves 6.

A good substitute for rice with chicken or pork.

You may substitute beef broth for chicken broth if desired, and serve with beef.

And you thought barley was just for soup?

Green Bean Casserole

---

2 pkg. frozen French-style green beans
1 can water chestnuts, drained and sliced
1 can (19 oz.) bean sprouts, drained well
3–4 green onions, chopped
1 can cream of mushroom soup
1 c. grated sharp cheese
1 can French-fried onion rings
   or chow mein noodles,
   or 1 c. of chopped almonds

Cook green beans for half of the cooking time and drain well.

In a large greased casserole, layer green beans, water chestnuts, bean sprouts, green onions, mushroom soup and cheese.

Bake for 30 min. at 350 degrees.

Sprinkle French-fried onion rings or noodles or almonds on top and bake 5 min. longer.

This casserole may be made ahead of time and refrigerated.

Serves 8.

Green Beans and Mushrooms

1 lb. frozen French-style green beans
1 can sliced mushrooms, drained
1 can cream of mushroom soup
½ c. milk or cream
salt and pepper to taste
2 tbsp. butter
1 c. bread crumbs
½ c. grated parmesan cheese

Cook frozen beans according to package instructions, just until tender-crisp.

Grease a 1-½-qt. casserole.

Mix beans with mushrooms and mushroom soup that has been thinned with the milk or cream, salt and pepper.

Place all in a casserole.

Melt butter in frying pan. Add bread crumbs and parmesan cheese. Top casserole with crumb topping.

Bake at 350 degrees for 45 min., or until heated through.

Serves 6.

Green Beans Oriental

3 stalks celery, cut diagonally into ½-in. slices
2 tbsp. butter or margarine
1 tbsp. cornstarch
¾ c. chicken broth
2 tbsp. soy sauce
2 tsp. toasted sesame seeds
dash garlic salt
2 cans (each 14 oz.) cut green beans, well drained,
    or 2 lb. frozen green beans, cooked as directed
    and well drained

Cook celery in butter or margarine until tender-crisp.

Blend cornstarch with chicken broth, soy sauce, sesame seeds and garlic salt.

Cook with the celery, stirring constantly, until thickened.

Add beans and heat thoroughly.

(Could be made ahead and placed in greased casserole dish and heated for 30 min. at 350 degrees.)

Serves 6–8.

Good with chicken and turkey.

Oktoberfest Beans

8 slices bacon
1 c. finely diced celery
1 c. finely diced onion
1 can (5-½ oz.) tomato paste
½ c. brown sugar
1 envelope spaghetti sauce mix
2 tbsp. prepared mustard
1 tsp. garlic salt
2 tbsp. white vinegar
2 cans (each 14 oz.) lima beans, drained
1 can (14 oz.) kidney beans, drained
1 can (28 oz.) pork and beans

Cook bacon until crisp, drain and crumble.

Add celery and onion to 2 tbsp. bacon fat and sauté for 5 min.

Add 1 c. water and all other ingredients, except beans. Bring to a boil.

In a 3-qt. casserole, combine beans and bacon. Stir in tomato mixture.

Bake, uncovered, for 1 hr. at 350 degrees.

Serves 10.

We named them "Oktoberfest Beans," but we love them anytime served with anything!

Beets with Pineapple

2 tbsp. brown sugar
1 tbsp. cornstarch
¼ tsp. salt
1 small can pineapple tidbits
1 tbsp. butter or margarine
1 tbsp. lemon juice
1 can (14 oz.) sliced beets, drained,
    or 2 c. fresh beets, cooked and sliced

Combine brown sugar, cornstarch and salt in a saucepan. Stir in pineapple with juice.

Cook, stirring constantly, until mixture thickens and bubbles. Add butter or margarine, lemon juice and beets.

Cook over medium heat for 5 min.

Serves 4–5.

We love our beets plain, fresh from the garden, but this one is so easy and a gourmet veggie for beet lovers!

Broccoli Casserole

2 pkg. frozen chopped broccoli or 1 lb. fresh
1 can cream of mushroom soup
2 eggs, well beaten
1 medium onion, chopped
1 c. grated cheddar cheese
1-½ c. stuffing mix
¼ c. butter, melted

Cook broccoli slightly, drain and place in a greased 2-qt. casserole.

Combine soup, eggs and onion. Pour this mixture over the broccoli.

Sprinkle cheese on top.

Add stuffing mix to butter and put this on top.

Bake at 350 degrees for 30 min.

Serves 6–8.

Broccoli Onion Delight

1 lb. broccoli or 2 pkg. (each 10 oz.)
  frozen chopped broccoli
3 medium onions, quartered
¼ c. butter or margarine
2 tbsp. flour
salt and pepper to taste
1 c. milk
1 small pkg. cream cheese
½ c. grated cheddar cheese
1 c. bread crumbs

Cut broccoli into spears and cook in small amount of water until tender-crisp, or cook frozen broccoli as instructed on package, and drain.

Cook onions in small amount of water until tender and drain.

In saucepan, melt half of the butter or margarine. Blend in the flour, salt and pepper.

Add milk and cook, stirring constantly, until thickened. Blend in the cream cheese until smooth.

Places veggies in a 2-qt. casserole, pour sauce over and mix lightly. Top with cheddar cheese.

Melt remaining half of the butter or margarine, and mix with the bread crumbs. Sprinkle on top of casserole and bake at 350 degrees for 40 min. or until heated through.

Serves 6.

Margie's Broccoli Casserole

1 lb. fresh broccoli or 2 pkg. (each 10 oz.)
   frozen chopped broccoli
1 can cream of mushroom soup
1 small container (250 ml) sour cream
1 tbsp. minced onion
1 c. grated cheddar cheese
15 Ritz crackers, crushed

Cook broccoli just until tender-crisp. Drain well.

Mix with all other ingredients in a greased 2-qt. casserole and bake for 20 min. at 350 degrees.

Do not overbake.

Serves 6.

We doubled this recipe for a dinner party. Everyone loved Margie's *broccoli!*

Swiss Brussels Sprouts

3 pkg. (each 10 oz.) frozen brussels sprouts
   or 2 lb. fresh
1 c. chopped onion
¼ c. butter
2 c. finely chopped celery
3-½ tbsp. flour
1-⅔ c. hot milk
½ tsp. nutmeg
½ tsp. paprika
salt and pepper to taste
1-½ c. grated swiss cheese
⅔ c. seasoned bread crumbs
3 tbsp. slivered almonds
2 tbsp. butter, softened

Cook brussels sprouts in boiling salted water until barely tender. Drain and cut in half.

Sauté onion in ¼ c. butter until golden. Stir in celery and cook 5 min. more. Stir in flour and cook 3 min.

Remove from heat and gradually pour in milk, stirring constantly.

Return to heat and cook until thick. Add nutmeg, paprika, salt and pepper. Fold in brussels sprouts and swiss cheese.

Spoon into greased 2-qt. casserole and sprinkle with seasoned crumbs and almonds and dot with butter.

Bake at 375 degrees for 20–30 min. or until browned and bubbly.

Serves 8–10.

Cabbage Casserole

3-½ c. sliced cabbage
1 c. chopped celery
4 tbsp. butter or margarine

Cream Sauce:
3 tbsp. butter
3 tbsp. flour
1 c. milk
Topping:
crushed potato chips
2 tbsp. butter

Sauté cabbage and celery in the butter or margarine for 10 min.

Place in casserole.

Melt butter, add flour, add milk and cook until thickened.

Pour over cabbage mixture.

Top with potato chips and dot with butter.

Bake at 350 degrees for 45 min.

This recipe was given to us by our friend Margie, who hates cabbage but loved this!

Pennsylvania Dutch Red Cabbage

4 slices bacon
1 medium onion, chopped
1 medium red cabbage, shredded
1 red apple, unpeeled, cored and cubed
¼ c. brown sugar
¼ c. white vinegar
1 tbsp. ground cloves
salt and pepper to taste
½ tsp. caraway seed
¼ c. red wine

In large saucepan, sauté bacon until crisp.

Remove bacon and crumble, saving 2 tbsp. drippings.

To the 2 tbsp. drippings, add all the remaining ingredients, plus the crumbled bacon.

Cook, covered, over low heat, stirring occasionally, for 30 min.

Serves 12.

A local traditional dish—not just Oktoberfest fare!
If you like cabbage, you'll love *this one!*

Baked Carrot Casserole

6 medium carrots, grated
3 tbsp. butter
salt and pepper to taste
¾ tsp. white sugar

In a greased casserole, layer carrots, 1 tbsp. butter, salt and pepper, and ¼ tsp. sugar.

Layer 3 times until all ingredients are used.

Bake at 350° for 45 min.

Serves 6.

If you love plain buttered carrots, you will love this make-ahead casserole.

For every extra person, just grate one more carrot!

Brandied Carrots

---

24 baby carrots
1 oz. orange-flavoured liqueur or orange juice
3 oz. lemon juice
2 oz. brandy or rum
2 oz. honey
1 tbsp. chopped parsley

Place carrots in saucepan of cold water and bring to a boil. Simmer until tender. Drain.

Place in greased baking dish.

Blend together liqueur or orange juice, lemon juice, brandy or rum and honey and pour over carrots.

Bake for 15 min. at 350 degrees, basting often.

Sprinkle with parsley and serve.

Serves 6.

Mother always said, "carrots are good for your eyes." We say these carrots are good for your tummy!

Souper Glazed Carrots

2 tbsp. chopped onion
1 tbsp. chopped parsley
2 tbsp. butter
8 large carrots, cut in 1-in. pieces
1 can consommé
dash nutmeg

In a saucepan, cook onion and parsley in butter for 5 min.

Add remaining ingredients.

Cover and cook for 10 min.

Uncover and cook for 20 min. or until carrots are tender and sauce thickens and forms a glaze.

Serves 5–6.

A carrot, a turnip, a pea,
Is healthy as can be!

Scalloped Cauliflower

---

2 pkg. (each 10 oz.) frozen cauliflower
   or 1 large cauliflower
1 can cream of celery soup
½ c. milk
2 eggs, slightly beaten
1 c. grated cheddar cheese
¾ c. bread crumbs
¼ c. chopped parsley
¼ c. chopped pimiento
1 tbsp. minced onion
salt and pepper

Cook frozen cauliflower as directed, or cook fresh cauliflower in small amount of water until tender-crisp. Drain well.

Combine soup, milk and eggs. Stir in half of the cheddar cheese. Add bread crumbs, parsley, pimiento, onion and salt and pepper to taste.

Add drained cauliflower and stir into soup mixture.

Turn into baking dish or casserole and bake for 35 min. at 350 degrees.

Top with remaining cheddar cheese and bake for 5 min. longer.

Serves 6–8.

Souper Easy Cauliflower

1 medium cauliflower, or 2 pkg.
   (each 10 oz.) frozen cauliflower
1 can cream of mushroom soup
1 c. grated cheddar cheese
1 can whole mushrooms, drained (optional)

Cook cauliflower until tender-crisp.

Mix soup and cheese in a greased casserole and stir in cooked cauliflower and mushrooms, if using.

Bake for 20 min. at 350 degrees.

Cauliflower stays white during cooking when a piece of lemon peel or a little milk is added to the water.

When there's no time to make cheese sauce for your cauliflower, this is a life saver!

Baked Celery Casserole

4 c. celery, cut diagonally into bite-size pieces
1 can water chestnuts, drained and cut in half
½ c. diced pimiento (optional)
1 can cream of chicken soup
½ c. bread crumbs
1 tbsp. butter
slivered almonds

Mix celery, water chesnuts, pimiento, if using, and soup together and place in a greased casserole dish.

Sauté bread crumbs in butter and spoon on top.

Sprinkle with slivered almonds.

Bake, covered, at 350 degrees for 25 min., and then bake, uncovered, for 15 min.

Serves 6.

Cheesey Garden Casserole

1 pkg. (7-¼ oz.) long grain and wild rice
3 c. sliced zucchini
1 green pepper, sliced
1 medium onion, sliced
1 can sliced mushrooms, drained
2 c. spaghetti sauce
2 c. grated cheddar cheese
1 c. grated swiss cheese

Cook rice according to package directions.

Simmer sliced vegetables together until just tender.
Drain well.

Place one-half of rice in a greased casserole dish.

Spoon one-half of vegetables over rice.

Sprinkle with cheddar cheese and one-half of the spaghetti sauce.

Layer rice, vegetables and rest of spaghetti sauce again.

Top with swiss cheese.

Bake, uncovered, for 35 min. at 375 degrees.

Serves 10.

Our favourite veggie casserole! A real winner! Brings raves whether served with a steak or with a hamburger.

Baked Corn and Swiss Cheese

1 can (19 oz.) whole kernel corn, drained
1 small can evaporated milk
1 c. grated swiss cheese
2 beaten eggs
2-3 green onions, chopped
dash pepper
1 c. fresh bread crumbs
2 tbsp. butter, melted

Combine corn, evaporated milk, ¾ c. of the cheese, eggs, onion and dash of pepper.

Turn mixture into greased 1-qt. casserole.

Toss bread crumbs with butter and remaining ¼ c. of the cheese.

Sprinkle over corn mixture.

Bake for 30 min. at 350 degrees.

Serves 4–6.

A welcome change from plain canned corn. Almost a soufflé!

Baked Corn and Tomatoes

1 can (12 oz.) corn niblets
1 can (19 oz.) stewed tomatoes
½ green pepper, chopped
½ tsp. salt
¼ tsp. pepper
½ tsp. sugar
¾ c. fresh bread crumbs
1 tbsp. butter or margarine

Drain corn and tomatoes.

Mix chopped green pepper and seasonings with corn and tomatoes and pour into a greased 1-½-qt. casserole.

Sprinkle crumbs on top and dot with butter or margarine.

Bake for 30 min. at 350 degrees.

Serves 4.

Fast and easy! A great combination!

Eggplant Parmesan

1 medium eggplant, unpeeled, cut in ½-in. slices
1 egg, beaten
½ c. fine, dry bread crumbs
¼ c. oil
salt and pepper to taste
1 can (14 oz.) spaghetti sauce
2 c. grated mozzarella cheese
grated parmesan cheese

Use two pie plates—one for the beaten egg and one for the crumbs.

Dip eggplant slices into beaten egg and then into crumbs.

Heat oil and brown eggplant well on both sides.

Place slices in single layer in large baking pan and season with salt and pepper.

Pour spaghetti sauce over eggplant and top with the mozzarella cheese.

Sprinkle with parmesan cheese.

Bake for 30 min. at 350 degrees.

A nice, easy, versatile eggplant casserole.
Serve at your next barbecue!

Mushroom Mania

1-½ lb. mushrooms, sliced
6 slices white bread, buttered
½ c. chopped onion
½ c. chopped celery
½ c. chopped green pepper
½ c. mayonnaise
¾ tsp. salt
¼ tsp. pepper
2 eggs
1-½ c. milk
1 can cream of mushroom soup
croutons
grated cheddar cheese

Sauté mushrooms in butter until barely cooked.

Cube 3 slices of bread and arrange them in a casserole.

Combine mushrooms with the onion, celery, green pepper, mayonnaise, salt and pepper, and put the mixture on top of the bread.

Cube remaining 3 slices of bread and put them on the mushroom mixture.

Beat eggs with milk and pour over everything. Refrigerate at least 1 hr.

One hour before serving, pour soup over it and top with a sprinkling of croutons.

Bake at 300 degrees for 50 min. Sprinkle grated cheese on top. Bake 10 min. more.

Serves 6.

Honey Orange Parsnips

4 medium parsnips, peeled and sliced
3 tbsp. butter or margarine
1 tbsp. honey
1 tsp. grated orange rind
3 tbsp. orange juice

Cook parsnips in boiling water until tender-crisp. Drain.

Combine remaining ingredients and pour over parsnips.

Simmer, stirring occasionally, until sauce is reduced and parsnips are glazed.

Serves 4.

*If your family, like ours, rejects parsnips, try these—
they're marvellous!*

Canton Peas

2 pkg. (each 10 oz.) frozen peas
1 can sliced mushrooms, drained
1 can water chestnuts, drained and sliced
1 c. chopped green onion
¾ tsp. ginger
¼ tsp. nutmeg
1 c. chicken broth or consommé
2 tbsp. cornstarch
1 tsp. salt
⅛ tsp. pepper
⅛ tsp. garlic powder

In saucepan, separate peas.

Add mushrooms, water chestnuts, onion, ginger, nutmeg, and ¾ c. of the broth or consommé. Cover and simmer for 3–4 min.

In a cup, mix cornstarch and remaining ¼ c. of broth until smooth. Stir into peas.

Cook, stirring constantly, until liquid boils and thickens.

Add salt, pepper and garlic powder.

Serves 6–8.

Creamed Peas

---

2 tbsp. butter
2 tbsp. chopped green onion
1 tbsp. flour
1 tsp. sugar
pinch thyme
pinch nutmeg
½ tsp. salt
dash pepper
¾ c. milk
2 pkg. (each 10 oz.) frozen peas

Melt butter. Add onion and cook gently, stirring constantly, for 5 min.

Add flour, sugar, thyme, nutmeg, salt and pepper. Stir to blend and remove from heat.

Add milk, stir and return to moderate heat. Cook, stirring constantly, until boiling, thickened and smooth. Turn heat to low and cook, stirring occasionally, for 10 min.

Cook peas in boiling salted water until tender-crisp. Drain.

Stir in hot sauce.

Serves 6–8.

No veggie book is complete without creamed peas. Good on toast or served in tiny tart shells!

Quick Oven Peas

2 pkg. (each 10 oz.) frozen peas
1 can sliced mushrooms, drained
¼ c. chopped onion
2 tbsp. butter
¼ tsp. savory
1 tbsp. water
salt and pepper to taste

Place all ingredients in a 1-½-qt. casserole.

Cover and bake at 350 degrees for 40–45 min. or until peas are tender, stirring after 20 min.

Serves 8.

Quick Creamy Peas

1 pkg. (10 oz.) frozen peas
½ c. sour cream
pinch celery salt
pinch dry mustard
dash pepper

Cook and drain peas.

Stir in remaining ingredients.

Serves 4.

Sweet Potato Casserole

4 c. hot, mashed sweet potatoes
¼ c. butter or margarine
½ tsp. salt
¼ c. orange juice
2 c. miniature marshmallows

Combine sweet potatoes with butter or margarine, salt, orange juice and 1 c. of the marshmallows.

Place in a greased 1-½-qt. casserole.

Dot with remaining marshmallows and bake at 350 degrees for 30 min.

Hash Brown Potato Casserole

1 can cream of mushroom soup
   or cream of chicken soup
1 large carton (500 ml) sour cream
¼ c. margarine, melted
2 c. grated cheddar cheese
2 lb. frozen hash brown potatoes
1 c. diced onion
crushed potato chips

Place soup, sour cream, margarine and cheese in saucepan and simmer, stirring, until well blended.

Mix with frozen hash brown potatoes and onion.

Place in very large, greased casserole or two smaller ones.

Sprinkle with potato chips and bake in 375 degree oven for 1 hr.

Serves 12.

We've made these hash browns for years! Try them with your Easter ham or your next champagne breakfast. Try them in a foil pan on your barbecue!

Make-Ahead Mashed Potatoes

9 large potatoes
1 large pkg. (250 g) cream cheese, softened
1 c. sour cream
2 tsp. onion salt
1 tsp. salt
dash pepper
2 tbsp. butter
1 egg, beaten

Cook potatoes in boiling water until tender. Drain.

Mash well and add the rest of the ingredients.
Beat until fluffy.

Let cool slightly and place in large, greased casserole.
Dot with more butter and refrigerate.

To serve, remove from the refrigerator 1 hr. before serving
and bake, uncovered, at 350 degrees for 30 min. or until
heated through.

Serves 12.

This may be prepared 5 days ahead and refrigerated until
ready to use.

May also be frozen, but thaw completely before heating.

*No last-minute mashing! Even mashed potatoes may be made
ahead!*

Mary Ellen's Cheese and Potato Bake

4 medium potatoes, boiled
salt and pepper to taste
2 large tomatoes
1 tsp. dried basil
½ lb. mozzarella cheese, grated
⅓ c. chopped parsley
⅓ c. grated parmesan cheese
¼ c. melted butter

Cut potatoes in ½-in. slices and arrange in single layer in greased 9 x 13 baking pan.

Season with salt and pepper.

Slice tomatoes and arrange on top of potatoes.

Sprinkle with basil and more salt and pepper to taste.

Top with mozzarella cheese, parsley and parmesan cheese.

Drizzle melted butter over all.

Bake at 350 degrees for 25 min.

Serves 6.

Oven French Fries for Two

1 large potoato, unpeeled
1 tbsp. oil
dash salt
dash pepper
dash paprika

Heat oven to 450–475 degrees.

Scrub potato and cut in half lengthwise.

Cut each half into 8 fingers and toss fingers in oil.

Place on cookie sheet, not touching.

Baked for 20–25 min., turning once.

Sprinkle with salt, pepper and paprika.

Too good for two!
Make more—you'll never buy frozen again!

Fanny's Sweet Potato Casserole

3 c. mashed sweet potatoes
    or 3 large sweet potatoes, cooked and mashed
⅓ c. half and half cream or milk
½ c. butter
⅔ c. white sugar
2 eggs, slightly beaten
1 tsp. vanilla
Topping:
1 c. brown sugar
½ c. flour
⅓ c. melted butter
1 c. chopped pecans

Mix sweet potatoes, cream or milk, butter, sugar, eggs and vanilla and pour into a greased casserole.

Mix topping ingredients together with a fork.

Sprinkle topping mixture on sweet potatoes.

Bake at 350 degrees for 30–35 min.

Serves 6.

Use less sugar if you like—but don't tell Fanny!

Yams and Pommes

---

2 cans sweet potatoes
 or 6 medium sweet potatoes
2 medium tart apples
½ c. brown sugar
salt and pepper to taste
¾ tsp. nutmeg
½ tsp. cinnamon
¼ c. melted butter
½ c. orange juice
2 tbsp. lemon juice
1 tbsp. prepared mustard
⅓ c. seedless raisins
⅓ c. chopped pecans

Slice canned sweet potatoes, or cook fresh sweet potatoes until tender, drain and slice.

Pare, core and slice apples.

In a greased casserole, layer potatoes and then apples, sprinkling each layer with sugar, salt, pepper, nutmeg and cinnamon.

Repeat layers, ending with apples.

Mix butter, orange juice, lemon juice and mustard. Pour over top.

Sprinkle with raisins and pecans.

Bake at 350 degrees for 40 min.

Serves 8.

Carol's Spinach Ricotta Pie

2 green onions, chopped
2 tbsp. butter
1 bag spinach, washed, drained and broken,
    or 1 pkg. (10 oz.) frozen spinach, cooked and
    drained well
3 eggs
½ c. light cream
1 c. ricotta cheese
½ c. grated farmer's or mild cheese
salt and pepper to taste
1 9-in. unbaked pie shell

Sauté onions in butter. Add spinach and sauté.

Beat eggs, cream, ricotta and mild cheese together.

Add spinach mixture and salt and pepper, and beat with electric mixer.

Pour into pie shell and bake at 375 degrees for 30 min.

You may top with more mild cheese, if desired.

Serves 6.

Laurel's Spinach Casserole

1 pkg. (10 oz.) frozen spinach or 1 bag fresh
½ c. sour cream
¼ pkg. dry onion soup mix
1 egg, slightly beaten

Partially cook spinach and drain well.

Mix sour cream, dry onion soup mix and slightly beaten egg together and fold in spinach.

Bake in a greased casserole for 30 min. at 350 degrees.

Serves 4.

Laurel says this is a great way to get your kids to eat their spinach!

Spinach and Mushrooms

2 bags spinach
¾–1 lb. mushrooms
3 tbsp. bacon fat or cooking oil
1-½ c. grated cheddar cheese
¼ c. sherry

Wash and trim spinach. Place in a large saucepan and bring to a boil. Cook 5 min. and drain well.

Wash and slice mushrooms and sauté in bacon fat or oil for 10 min.

Layer spinach, mushrooms, cheese and sherry in a 2-qt. greased casserole until all ingredients are used, ending with a layer of cheese and sherry.

Bake, uncovered, for 30 min. at 350 degrees.

Serves 6.

Popeye loves spinach—now you will too!

Yellow Squash Casserole

2 lb. yellow squash, sliced
1 large onion, chopped
1 can cream of chicken soup
1 c. sour cream
1 tsp. salt
¼ tsp. pepper
2 large carrots, grated
¼ c. butter or margarine, melted
8 oz. seasoned bread crumbs
paprika (optional)

In saucepan cook squash and onion in boiling salted water until tender. Drain. May be mashed or left in slices.

Combine soup, sour cream, salt and pepper. Mix well.

Stir in carrots. Fold in squash and onion.

Combine butter and seasoned crumbs.

Sprinkle half of the crumb mixture in a greased 2-½-qt. casserole, pour squash mixture over and top with remaining crumb mixture. Or pour squash mixture into casserole and top with buttered crumbs. Sprinkle with paprika and bake at 350 degrees for 30-45 min. or until heated through.

Really good! The best squash casserole we tried.

Marilyn's Scalloped Tomatoes and Herbs

2 medium onions, sliced
1-½ tsp. sugar
½ tsp. salt
¼ tsp. pepper
½ tsp. thyme
¼ c. butter, melted
1 can (28 oz.) tomatoes
2 c. coarse, fresh bread crumbs
1 tsp. chopped chives
2 tbsp. chopped parsley
2 tbsp. butter, softened

Sauté onions, sugar, salt, pepper and thyme in ¼ c. butter until onions are transparent.

Drain tomatoes and chop.

Mix bread crumbs, chives and parsley, and add one-half of this mixture to the onions.

Layer tomatoes and onion mixture, ending with tomatoes.

Top with the other half of the crumb mixture and dot with the 2 tbsp. butter.

Bake uncovered at 350 degrees for 45 min.

Top should be crispy.

Stuck for a veggie? Goes well with everything!

Festive Turnip

1 large turnip
2 tbsp. butter
2 cooking apples (courtland or spy)
¼ c. brown sugar
dash cinnamon

Topping:
⅓ c. brown sugar
⅓ c. flour
2 tbsp. cold butter

Peel and dice turnip. Cook in boiling water until tender. Drain and mash with butter.

Peel and slice apples and mix with the brown sugar and cinnamon.

In a greased casserole, layer half the turnip, then the apple and then the remaining turnip.

Put brown sugar and flour in a small bowl and cut in the butter until crumbly. Sprinkle on top of turnip and bake at 350 degrees for 1 hr.

Serves 8.

This is our traditional Christmas dinner turnip.

Turnips and Veggies Au Gratin

1-¼ c. boiling water
1 tsp. salt
1 small turnip, cut into strips
1 large onion, quartered
1 c. celery, cut into ½-in. slices
½ green pepper, cut into strips
2 tbsp. cornstarch
¼ c. cold water
½ c. grated cheddar cheese
1 tbsp. butter

Bring water to boil and add salt. Add turnip and onion and cook gently, covered, for 15 min. Then add celery and green pepper and cook until all are tender-crisp.

Drain and reserve liquid in another pot. Keep drained vegetables warm. (You should have 1 c. of drained liquid.)

Stir cornstarch with cold water and make a paste. Add to reserved liquid.

Stir in cheese and butter over medium heat. Stir until melted and add veggies.

Heat thoroughly.

Serves 6.

A little more effort, but well worth it!

Veggie Moussaka

1 medium eggplant
1 tsp. salt
½ c. vegetable oil
3 medium zucchini
2 medium onions
2 cloves garlic, minced
1 can (28 oz.) whole tomatoes
salt and pepper to taste
½ lb. penne noodles
¼ c. milk
1 egg, slightly beaten
½ c. grated parmesan cheese
2 tbsp. parsley
2 c. grated mozzarella or swiss cheese

Peel eggplant and slice into ¼-in. slices. Place on oiled cookie sheet, sprinkle with salt and drizzle with ¼ c. of the oil. Broil until golden. Turn and brown the other side. Remove and set aside.

Slice zucchini lengthwise into ¼-in. slices. Place on cookie sheet and drizzle with remaining ¼ c. oil. Brown until golden. Turn and brown the other side. Remove and set aside.

Brown onions and garlic in small amount of oil until transparent. Remove and set aside.

Drain tomatoes, reserving juice. Slice tomatoes. Add salt and pepper to juice.

Cook noodles according to package directions and drain.

Mix milk with beaten egg and pour over cooked noodles. Mix well.

In a greased 9 x 13 baking dish, layer noodle mixture, parmesan cheese, eggplant, onion mixture, parsley, zucchini, sliced tomatoes, tomato juice and mozzarella or swiss cheese.

Bake at 350 degrees for 30 min.

Serves 12.

A little more preparation but well worth the effort!

Veggie Spaghetti Sauce

2 large ripe tomatoes, chopped
1 small onion, chopped
1 c. diced zucchini (1 small)
1 c. diced eggplant
1 medium red pepper, sliced,
    or 1 medium green pepper, sliced, or both
2 cloves garlic, finely chopped
¼ c. olive oil
2 tbsp. butter
1 c. meatless spaghetti sauce
1 lb. spaghetti
salt and pepper
grated parmesan cheese

Sauté tomatoes, onion, zucchini, eggplant, red pepper or green pepper, or both, and garlic in oil and butter on medium heat for 10 min. or until veggies are tender.

Add spaghetti sauce to veggies and simmer for 10 min.

Meanwhile, cook spaghetti according to package directions and drain.

Season with salt and pepper.

Serve sauce over warm spaghetti and sprinkle with parmesan cheese.

Serves 4-6.

We all loved this meatless spaghetti sauce! A vegetarian's delight!

Stuffed Zucchini

4 medium zucchini
1-¾ c. fresh bread crumbs
½ c. grated cheddar cheese
¼ c. chopped onion
2 tbsp. chopped parsley
salt and pepper to taste
2 eggs, beaten
¼ tsp. salt
2 tbsp. butter
½ c. grated parmesan cheese

Scrub zucchini well. Cut off ends but do not peel.

Cook in 2 c. boiling salted water. Do not overcook. Drain.

Cut zucchini in half lengthwise and carefully remove centre part with tip of a spoon.

Turn zucchini hollow side down on paper towels to drain.

Chop centre part of zucchini and combine with crumbs, cheddar cheese, onion, parsley, salt, pepper and eggs.

Place zucchini hollow side up in a greased 9 x 13 baking pan. Sprinkle with salt.

Fill with bread mixture. Dot with butter and sprinkle with parmesan cheese. Bake at 350 degrees for 35–45 min, or until browned on top.

Serves 8.

Tomato Zucchini Casserole

1 c. grated cheddar cheese
⅓ c. grated parmesan cheese
1 tsp. chopped fresh oregano or ½ tsp. dried
1 tsp. chopped fresh basil or ½ tsp. dried
1 clove garlic, minced
½ tsp. salt
¼ tsp. freshly ground pepper
3 medium zucchini, sliced
2 large tomatoes, sliced
¼ c. butter
2 tbsp. finely chopped onions
½ c. bread crumbs

Combine cheddar cheese, parmesan cheese, herbs, garlic, salt and pepper.

Grease a 2-qt. casserole.

Arrange half of the zucchini slices in casserole. Sprinkle with one-quarter of the cheese mixture.

Arrange half of sliced tomatoes on top and sprinkle with one-quarter of cheese mixture.

Repeat layers with remaining zucchini, one-quarter of cheese mixture, remaining tomatoes and remaining cheese mixture.

In a small skillet, melt butter and sauté onions until transparent. Add bread crumbs and stir until they absorb butter. Spread on top of casserole.

Cover and bake at 375 degrees for 30 min. Uncover and bake 20–25 min. or until top is crusty and vegetables are tender.

Serves 6.